B

Be a Creative Writer

Tish Farrell

Your writing mission

Do you want to tell exciting real-life stories? Do you long to discover
lost cities in Amazon jungles? Could you dog-sled across Arctic wastes?
Would you like to travel back in time: be a medieval knight?
Do enchanted lands with wizards and elves capture your
imagination? Do you think you could solve perplexing mysteries?
Or do space ships and aliens take your fancy?

This book will teach you to write any of these stories
and more - - your imagination is the only limit.

Your mission is to find your own stories to tell. To help you on your
way, there will be all kinds of brainstorming exercises and writers'
tips that will develop your creative writing skills. There will be hints
from famous writers and examples from their books to inspire you.

But don't forget! Becoming a good writer takes lots of time
and practice. There are no short cuts to reach your goal.

Now, get ready for the exciting writing quest ...

Good luck!

ISBN: 978-1-84898-204-8 pbk
This compilation published in 2010 by *ticktock* Entertainment Ltd

Printed in China
9 8 7 6 5 4 3 2 1

Copyright © *ticktock* Entertainment Ltd 2006, 2010
First published in Great Britain as part of the series *Write Your Own* in 2006 by *ticktock* Media Ltd, The Old Sawmill, 103 Goods Station
Road, Tunbridge Wells, Kent, TN1 2DP

NOTE TO READERS
The website addresses are correct at the time of publishing. However, due to the ever-changing nature of
the internet, websites and content may change. Some websites can contain links that are unsuitable for
children. The publisher is not responsible for changes in content or website addresses. We advise that
internet searches should be supervised by an adult.

CONTENTS

WHY DO WRITERS WRITE?

No writer would say that writing is easy. Most well-known writers will have toiled for years before seeing their first stories in print. They write to tell a story that must be told and because they believe that nothing is more important than stories.

Brian Jacques

Brian Jacques (below right) wrote his first story at the age of ten. His teacher said it was so good that he couldn't possibly have written it. He left school at 15 and did many jobs, but it was while he was a milkman that he wrote his first *Redwall* story to read out to the children there. His old English teacher secretly sent a copy of this story off to a publisher, and that is how he won a contract to write the first five books in the *Tales of Redwall* series. His advice: 'Remember that television can't take you places the way that books can. So read, read, read.'

Christopher Paolini

Christopher Paolini was still a teenager when his first book *Eragon* was published to much acclaim. He says writers need to write about what excites them most, or they won't have the enthusiasm to write a whole novel – 'be persistent; be disciplined; be humble enough to accept editorial criticism; learn everything you can about the writer's craft.'

J. K. Rowling

J. K. Rowling (left) wrote her first story when she was five or six. It was about a rabbit called Rabbit, and from then on, she knew she only wanted to be a writer. All the same, it was only when she was grown up and bringing up her own small daughter that she finally finished her first *Harry Potter* novel. It took her five years to write. This wasn't her first book either. She had already written and put aside two novels for adults. Rowling says: 'being able to say I was a published author was the fulfilment of a dream.'

Philip Pullman

Pullman (right) goes to his desk every day at 9.30 a.m. and works until lunch time. He writes by hand and aims to write three sides of A4 paper. If he reaches this target, he spends the afternoon woodworking or playing the piano. If he hasn't, he goes back to his desk until he has. He always finishes his last sentence, or writes a new one, at the top of the fourth sheet – so he won't be faced with a blank page when he starts work the next day. He says: 'a lot of the time you're going to be writing without inspiration. The trick is to write just as well without it as with it.'

Margaret Mahy

Margaret sets her stories in her New Zealand homeland. She started writing when she was seven, but she was 33 and working as a librarian before she published her first stories. She knows it is rare for writers to have success with their first book. They all spend a lot of time working really hard and having their work rejected by publishers before they are published. Margaret says: 'Know within yourself why certain books work well for you.'

Terry Pratchett

Famous for his *Discworld* books, Terry published his first Sci-Fi story in his school magazine when he was 13. Two years later he was published professionally in the magazine *Science Fantasy*. He says this: 'We're living in science fiction, but we don't realize it. I was buying something for my wife in Perth, Australia, last time I was on tour. I couldn't remember her size, so I phoned her up … That is a science fiction conversation! All the more so for being mundane. I'm actually making a phone call all around the world on my mobile phone, to ask my wife her dress size!'

L. Frank Baum

He wrote *The Wonderful Wizard of Oz* – but had something to say about all forms of writing: 'Imagination has given us the steam engine, the telephone, the talking machine, and the automobile, for these things had to be dreamed of before they became realities. So I believe that dreams – day dreams … with your eyes wide open … are likely to lead to the betterment of the world.'

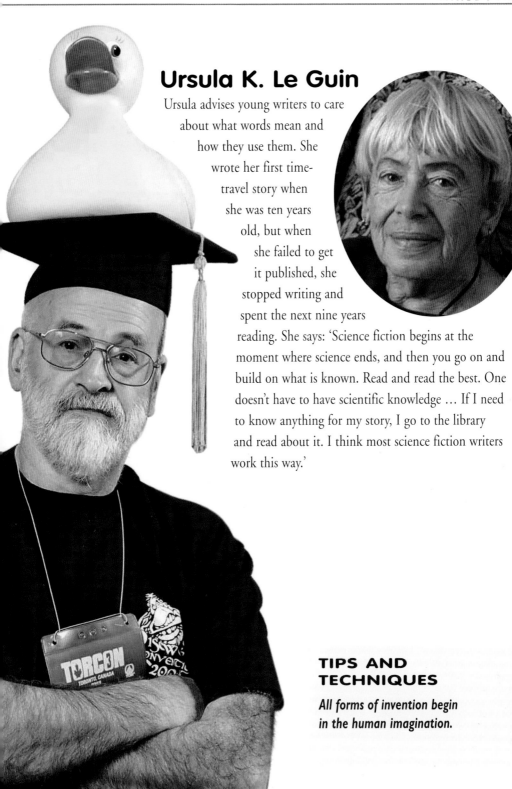

Ursula K. Le Guin

Ursula advises young writers to care about what words mean and how they use them. She wrote her first time-travel story when she was ten years old, but when she failed to get it published, she stopped writing and spent the next nine years reading. She says: 'Science fiction begins at the moment where science ends, and then you go on and build on what is known. Read and read the best. One doesn't have to have scientific knowledge ... If I need to know anything for my story, I go to the library and read about it. I think most science fiction writers work this way.'

TIPS AND TECHNIQUES

All forms of invention begin in the human imagination.

FIRST THINGS FIRST

First gather your writing materials and find your story-making place. Writers are lucky. They can write wherever they please, as long as they have a pen and paper. A computer can make writing quicker, but is not essential.

❶ Gather your writing materials

The following materials will help you organize your thoughts as you learn your craft and do your research at the library or on the Internet.

- A pocket notebook that you carry everywhere.
- Large spiral-bound notebooks and scrap paper.
- Pencils and pens with different coloured ink.
- Post-it notes for research ideas.
- Stick-on stars for highlighting stunning thoughts.
- Folders for storing up good story ideas.
- Dictionary, thesaurus and encyclopaedia.
- A camera to capture real people and places for your research.

❷ Create a writing place

Next you need to decide where your writing zone will be. Jacqueline Wilson writes on trains between schools visits. Judy Blume has a writing shack on an island. David Almond writes in a spare bedroom and on trains too. Your bedroom may be the best place, or the library where you can watch people while you work.

❸ Create a writing zone

- Play music that makes you feel calm and thoughtful;

- Make a collection of striking images of people and places;

- Have a hat or jacket that you only wear when you're writing;

- Choose some special objects to have around you while you work – a pen you use only for creative writing; maybe a snow dome (to shake up your ideas).

TIPS AND TECHNIQUES

Once you have found your writing place, the golden rule of becoming a real writer is: Go there as often as possible, and write something!

❹ Get in training

Before astronauts head for the stars, they must undergo long training programmes to prepare them for conditions in space. Becoming a writer is very like this. Don't just write when you feel like it. If all writers did this there would be far fewer books on the planet.

Now it's your turn

Learn to unlock your imagination

Try this brainstorming exercise. Have pens and scrap paper ready, plus a timer. Sit quietly in your writing zone for a few moments. Set the timer for two minutes and write the phrase 'space-time continuum' at the top of the paper. Now, without taking the pen from the page, you are going to write all the science fiction words, phrases and names you first think of. Don't worry about spelling or if it's rubbish. SPLURGE like a meteor shower! Then stop when two minutes are up. Brilliant! You've proved you can write.

MARTIAN   KRYPTONITE

SPACEMAN METEOR

ALIEN

❺ Reward yourself!

When you've finished the previous task, give yourself a gold star. You are on your way to finding the 'Lost Mines of Your Imagination'. The more you do exercises like this, the easier it will be to overcome the writer's worst enemy – the Story Spectre. The voice in your head that continually picks fault with your writing, also called your internal critic.

TIPS AND TECHNIQUES

Keep all your brainstorming notes in a file or notebook. You will need them later. Don't stop your writing practice. Fix a time slot and stick to it.

Case study

When Canadian Sci-Fi writer Robert J. Sawyer was in high school he started a Sci-Fi addicts club. With fellow members, he wrote scripts for a radio drama series that was never made. Later, Sawyer cut out all ideas that hadn't been his and shaped his first saleable story called 'Motive'. Many of the ideas in this first story – a murderous computer and dinosaur-like aliens – were developed in his later novels, including his first novel *The Golden Fleece*.

❻ **See how characters are used**

In mystery stories, the central character usually uses their deductive powers to right wrongs and prove that crime does not pay. These must be people that readers meet in the story. There may be one or more main suspects, but their motives (reasons) for doing wrong must be believable. They must also have the opportunity and realistic means to carry out their crime.

Case study

In 1930, Laura Ingalls Wilder couldn't find a publisher for her autobiography *Pioneer Girl*, so she used parts of it to create the first book of the much-loved *Little House* series – *Little House in the Big Woods*. This story is based on Laura's pioneering life in the big woods of Wisconsin during the late 19th century. Because the writer changed some of the facts, it is called historical fiction rather than autobiography.

TIPS AND TECHNIQUES

Make a regular date with your writing desk. Your practice may be five minutes or an hour. The trick is to stick to it.

Now it's your turn

A slice of time

Think about your favourite historical event. Imagine a time machine has taken you back there. Close your eyes and try to visualize it. What can you feel, hear, smell, touch and see? Take ten minutes to write down all your first thoughts. Don't worry about complete sentences. Scribble down every impression, even if it seems silly. This is about becoming a writer, not about being the best writer.

TIPS AND TECHNIQUES

Don't let anything put you off your writing. Even two minutes' practice a day is better than none and the more you write, the better you will become.

❼ Keep going

The more you do exercises like these, the easier it will be to defeat the Story Spectre – your internal critic who says your writing is useless. Try these storylines at practice time:

• *The day my house burned down and I became homeless.*

• *My most embarrassing experience.*

• *My best and worst birthdays.*

❽ Brainstorm

If writers get stuck, they can sometimes solve the problem using exciting sentences to spark off ideas. For example:

• *The day it rained broomsticks.*

• *How I turned my gerbil/cat/labrador into a handsome prince and the terrible trouble it caused my family.*

Brainstorming with a friend can be fun. You may come up with ideas that might never have occurred to you on your own.

❾ Make reading enjoyable

Grow your imagination. But if you are not enjoying a book, leave it and start another. Make a note of why you didn't like it. You might find this information useful later. Make sure you read a mix of genres – you may assume you don't like science fiction but have you actually read any? Try reading non-fiction too.

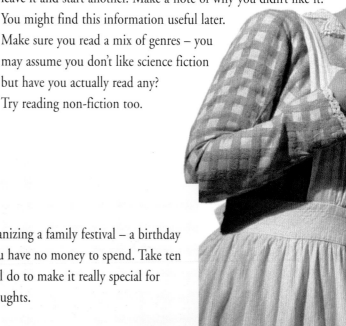

Now it's your turn

Making real-life magic

Imagine you are in charge of organizing a family festival – a birthday or a religious celebration. But you have no money to spend. Take ten minutes to describe what you will do to make it really special for everyone. Jot down your first thoughts.

Case studies

Louisa May Alcott's *Little Women*, published in 1868, is based on her own impoverished family life. The book's straightforward style has made it a bestseller ever since. Charles Dickens knew all about hard times. His own father was sent to a debtors' prison, and the writer used these experiences when he wrote *Little Dorrit*. After leaving school he worked for a law firm, recording court proceedings, and then as a parliamentary journalist. He had the best possible practice for becoming one of the world's greatest writers of fiction.

TIPS AND TECHNIQUES

The key to writing good fiction is to tell a believable story from an unexpected angle. Think personal and look to the heart of things as you write.

➊ Learn from the masters

After the mystery is revealed in a mystery book, the story goes on to reconstruct the events that explain it. Readers are given clues, which piece together like a jigsaw to solve the mystery. Cunning writers may lay several red herrings or false clues, but the ending must be both satisfying and surprising. So, if you'd like to write a mystery story, read as many different kinds of mystery as possible. They won't all fit this mystery blueprint, but find the ones that intrigue you most. Look at how the writers drop clues. If a good character starts to form in your mind, make notes.

➊ Discover your tastes

Think more deeply about the books you like. Are they set in totally different worlds with wizards and magic forces, like J. R. R. Tolkien's *The Lord of the Rings* (right)? Or do you like the story to move back and forth between real and imagined places as in C. S. Lewis' *The Chronicles of Narnia?* Or do you prefer something comic, set in the real world, such as Roald Dahl's *Matilda?*

➊ Look more deeply

Go back to a favourite story and, as you read, imagine that you are writing it. Start looking for the things that make that world so believable. When you first read it you probably lost yourself in it, and forgot all about the real world.

⓭ Get inspiration from myths and legends

Have you noticed that many stories draw their ideas from other stories? *The BFG, The Wonderful Wizard of Oz* (right), *The Hobbit, His Dark Materials* trilogy – all have their roots in ancient myths and fairy tales. Tolkien may have had Merlin in mind when he created Gandalf.

⓮ Create illusions

As a trainee writer, you want to discover why and how stories work. This is rather like trying to spot how a magician performs his tricks. Story writing is all about creating illusions. So, as you study your best-loved stories, look for the particular things that made you think that somewhere, in some other place, space or time, the magic worlds described in them really did exist.

TIPS AND TECHNIQUES

As you read, think about whose story you want to tell. What kind of world do they live in? Write everything down in your notebook and, when you come to write your story, you will have plenty of characters and places to choose from. Keep inspired and the ideas will flow ...

A WRITER'S VOICE

You've discovered that becoming a good writer means being a good reader. This is the only way to discover your own writer's voice – a style of writing that is uniquely yours. It is not something you learn quickly, which is why writing practice is so important. Writers go on developing their voices all their lives.

❶ Find your voice

Once you start reading with a writer's mind, you will notice that writers have their own rhythm and range of language. For instance, Sharon Creech (author of *The Wanderer*) 'sounds' nothing like Michael Morpurgo (author of *Kensuke's Kingdom*).

❷ Experiment

Once you've found an author whose books you really enjoy, it's tempting to stick to them. Don't! Experiment. Once in a while read something quite different: a historical novel or a book of legends. You may be surprised what ideas it gives you.

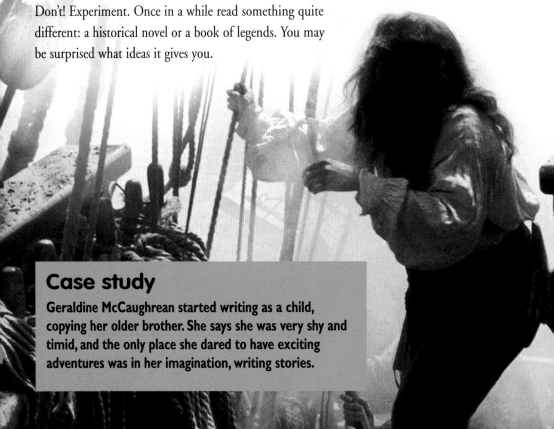

Case study

Geraldine McCaughrean started writing as a child, copying her older brother. She says she was very shy and timid, and the only place she dared to have exciting adventures was in her imagination, writing stories.

WRITERS' VOICES

Look at the kinds of words these authors use.
Do they use lots of adjectives? Are they good ones?
What about the length of their sentences? Do some
styles seem old fashioned? Do you think this matters?

Robert Louis Stevenson

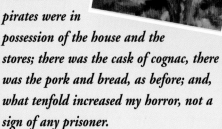

The glare of the torch, lighting up the interior of the block-house, showed me the worst of my apprehensions realized. The pirates were in possession of the house and the stores; there was the cask of cognac, there was the pork and bread, as before; and, what tenfold increased my horror, not a sign of any prisoner.

Robert Louis Stevenson, *Treasure Island*

Arthur C. Clarke

It was the last days of the Empire. The tiny ship was far from home, and almost a hundred light-years from the great parent vessel searching through the loosely packed stars at the rim of the Milky Way. But even here it could not escape from the shadow that lay across civilization.

Arthur C. Clarke, *Encounter at Dawn*

H. Rider Haggard

On we tramped silently as shades through the night and in the heavy sand. The karoo bushes caught our feet and retarded us, and the sand worked into our veldschoens and Good's shooting-boots, so that every few miles we had to stop and empty them.

H. Rider Haggard, *King Solomon's Mines*

Sharon Creech

We were racing along and it felt so terrific, all that wind! We had our foul-weather gear on, so we didn't mind the torrents of rain beating down as we ploughed through the water.

Sharon Creech, *The Wanderer*

❸ Don't panic!

If you are stuck for story ideas, don't panic! That will just make your brain go blank. In fact, you already have lots of ideas, locked away in the 'Lost Mines of Your Imagination'. This is where your subconscious memory stores every story experience you've ever had.

❹ Freeing your stories

The true writer's art is to extract all the brilliant story strands that are hidden in his or her head and to shape them into sparkling new tales. Brainstorming is a good way to start accessing your subconscious memory, but you'll probably need some extra tricks, too, before you can free your stories.

❺ Idea search

If you ask writers where they get their ideas they will say things like 'everywhere', or a character 'just came to them'. In fact, most writers such as Charles Dickens (left) store ideas for years, gathering information both consciously and subconsciously. Things get mixed up with memories and other stories and conversations they overhear. People they meet get mixed in too, along with newspaper articles, song lyrics, bits of poems. Everyone does this, but writers do it on purpose. Once in a while, something triggers a fully formed character or story.

Case study

Philip Pullman says he's stolen ideas from every book he's read. By this, he doesn't mean that he's copied what other writers have written. He means that his own story ideas are often inspired by memories of the things he has read: from comics to poetry to ancient stories.

Now it's your turn

Brainstorming

Speed up your ideas search with this brainstorming exercise. Cut up some scrap paper into ten squares (big enough to write one name on). Do the same with five different coloured sheets of paper, so you end up with six piles of ten squares. Now you are going to write, as fast as you can, the first thoughts that come into your mind. On your first pile of squares, write the names of ten possible heroes (or protagonists), one per square (e.g. Witchfinder-Elfgirl). The other piles are for: the main villain (or antagonist) (e.g. Worst Witch); a name for your fantasy world or a part of it (e.g. Heights of Horus); a magical object that will be important in the story (e.g. Truth Wand); a hero's helper (e.g. Silver Falcon); and a villain's henchman (e.g. Man-eating Cat). Now shuffle each pile and place them face down on your writing desk. Turn over the top square from each pile. There! You now have the six vital ingredients for a fantasy story: heroes, villains, a place, and an object for them to battle over.

TIPS AND TECHNIQUES

Keep your brainstorming notes in your notebook or in a separate file. A lot of it may seem like nonsense now. But the next time you flick through, something may inspire you.

Case study

Michael Morpurgo bases all of his fiction on real life situations. He says: 'All my stories are based on truth of some sort, some nugget of reality. I need to have a face I recognize and put it in a book. I need to hear language. I need to have gone to the place about which I am writing.'

TIPS AND TECHNIQUES

You can brainstorm anywhere – when you are on the bus or even waiting for the dentist. Make lists – mental ones if you have no paper. 'How many words mean lost?' 'How many ways are there to describe a jungle?' 'Exotic place names.' 'Favourite heroes.' Exercises like this shake up your memories. Who knows what will pop out?

Now it's your turn

Personal experiences

Read the extracts opposite and copy out the one you like best. Does the piece remind you of something that has happened to you? If it does, write down your own story. Try writing it in a humorous style, and then in a tragic or sarcastic one.

WRITERS' VOICES

Look at the words these authors use. Think about the rhythm and length of sentences. Which style do you prefer?

Dodie Smith

I Capture the Castle begins with a most unusual opening:

I write this sitting in the kitchen sink. That is, my feet are in it; the rest of me is on the draining-board, which I have padded with our dog's blanket and the tea-cosy. I can't say that I am really comfortable…but this is the only part of the kitchen where there is any daylight left. And I have found that sitting in a place that you have never sat before can be inspiring – I wrote my very best poem while sitting on the hen-house.

Charles Dickens

In *Great Expectations*, escaped convict Magwitch ambushes the hero Pip:

A man started up from among the graves at the side of the church porch.

'Keep still you little devil, or I'll cut your throat!'

A man who had been soaked in water, and smothered in mud, and lamed by stones, and cut by flints, and stung by nettles, and torn by briars; who limped, and shivered, and glared and growled; and whose teeth chattered in his head as he seized me by the chin.

Sharon Creech

In *Heartbeat*, Annie tells the story of her life in poems:

Sometimes when I am running a boy appears like my sideways shadow from the trees he emerges running falling into thump-thump steps beside me.

❻ Get researching

Having a story idea is just the start. Next comes much research while you develop the idea into a story. You will need some facts and some real-world information to grow a good story. Start the gathering process. Note down any good ideas or interesting information in your notebook. Maybe you can use your own interests or special knowledge – of computer games, sport, astronomy – to develop some future scenario. Making your story scientifically accurate is a great way to grab your reader's attention and bring them into your world.

❼ Where to look

- Search for related articles in the popular press.

- Look out for doom-and-gloom headlines.

- Look for direct quotes. What awful or extraordinary things have happened to people? Their words might trigger your own characters.

- Search for more specialist articles in the national press or on media websites. CNN and BBC News have good popular coverage.

- Read popular science journals: *Science News*, *New Scientist*, *National Geographic*, *Astronomy* etc.

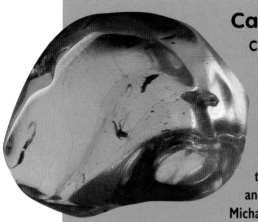

Case study

Canadian writer Robert J. Sawyer uses *Science News* for his science facts. It was here that he read about prehistoric mosquitoes trapped in amber and the possibility of dinosaur blood being preserved in their bellies. Could it be used to clone dinosaurs? the article posed. 'Neat!' he thought and turned the page. When writer Michael Crichton read the same article, he thought, 'Ye-ees!' It prompted him to write *Jurassic Park*.

TIPS AND TECHNIQUES

Start a dream diary to tap into your subconscious mind. Have a notebook beside your bed and write down any dream ideas as soon as you wake up.

Now it's your turn

Building worlds

Once your story ideas start simmering, you can help things along by building the physical world where your story will take place. Repeat the brainstorming exercise on page 10. See if it has taken more shape. Can you feel your ideas developing? Do you need some more?

8 Do some star research

Writing from first-hand experience is hard to beat, but if you want to write about someone whose life you've only glimpsed, some serious research is called for to make your story believable. Suppose you want to write a story about a young film or rock star. Begin by reading about as many real stars as possible – Britney Spears or Macaulay Culkin (right), for example.

9 Gather information

Collect articles from celebrity magazines and newspapers. Look at stars' official sites on the Internet. Make notes on what they say about themselves and how they live. Write down the actual words they use. Research stars from past eras too, such as Shirley Temple and Judy Garland.

TIPS AND TECHNIQUES

Start a newspaper-cuttings file of intriguing stories. Collect the most dramatic stories (such as kids who have won despite all the odds) and cut out photos of interesting characters.

10 Build a fictional star's profile

Build up a celebrity profile based on several stars' lives. If you do your research well, you will find all the real-life conflict and drama you need to make an interesting story.

Now it's your turn

A perfect recipe?

Cut scrap paper into 80 'cards' and divide them into four equal piles. Take five minutes to brainstorm options for each pile – 20 characters, 20 locations, 20 objects and 20 proverbs/sayings (pick some from a book if you can't think of 20). Shuffle the piles and deal yourself one card from each pile. You now have four ingredients to make a story. For ten minutes, brainstorm your first thoughts about how they come together and what happens.

⑪ Ask questions

Ask questions and more questions to find your story. What are a young star's problems? Do they worry about their looks and develop an eating disorder? Do they long for a true friend? Do they want a different career? Asking questions will help you to see their story.

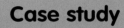

Case study

Jack Gantos created the *Joey Pigza* trilogy after meeting children with attention deficit hyperactivity disorder on his schools visits. One night he was writing about a particular boy in his diary and the character of Joey Pigza started coming to life. Gantos was inspired to write a story to show that children whose lives are managed by 'meds' are not bad kids.

⓬ Discover a setting

Now you need to create your story's setting. You must find ways to make it believable and it needs to work for your story. If you haven't planned it properly, your hero could end up stuck forever in a blind alley, simply because they have no believable way out!

⓭ Drop hints

If particular places or artefacts are going to be crucial to solving a mystery, then their existence must be established early on in the story. They must be part of the landscape that the reader can picture, though not in an obvious way.

Suppose a large marble urn in an old lady's grand house is a possible murder weapon. Early on the readers need to see it – but not see it. One way to do this, is to mention it in a list of other things, perhaps when your hero goes to tea. Later, when a victim is found apparently crushed by the urn, readers will think they know exactly what happened. But was it an accident, or made to look like one? Or will it turn out to be just another red herring?

TIPS AND TECHNIQUES

When brainstorming, don't forget to write top-of-the-head thoughts. Don't be afraid to write nonsense. It can lead to brilliant stuff. If you want to have a historical setting for your mystery, make sure you know your facts.

What an eerie place! I stepped through the door and a huge grizzly attacked me – all teeth and claws. It took me a moment to realize he was stuffed, but by then I'd swung round into a huge urn, which teetered and rocked on its stand. I steadied it just before it fell on me. All round the walls, grim antique faces sneered down at me.

Tish Farrell

⑭ Build a landscape

You can begin from a specific place and build the landscape around it, or work from a general landscape and zoom into a specific location later. You could draw a map of the area and use coloured stickers to highlight the story locations, eg crime scenes or dangerous places on your hero's quest. If your setting is real, then think how the local transport routes, parks and landmarks might serve your story.

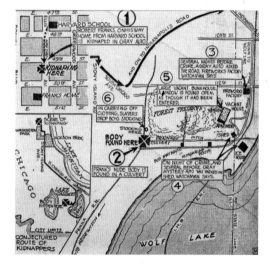

Now it's your turn

Be a real detective

It's time to do some legwork. Study places like the ones you want to use in your story. You could start with your own bedroom. Then there is your school, the museum, train station or park. Take a notebook. Imagine you're seeing the place for the first time. What do you notice: a particular smell or atmosphere; certain noises or textures? Each time do a two-minute brainstorm, noting five things you see, hear, feel and smell.

⓮ Building a world

World building is like writing a geography assignment and creating the geography too. But you can use magazines, books and computer games to imagine it better. Create a profile of your world. Draw maps and plans. Think yourself into it: What is there? How do people live and travel around? What are their houses like? What do people wear, eat? Are there aliens, robots, elves, dwarves, tigers, elephants?

⓰ Make your setting real

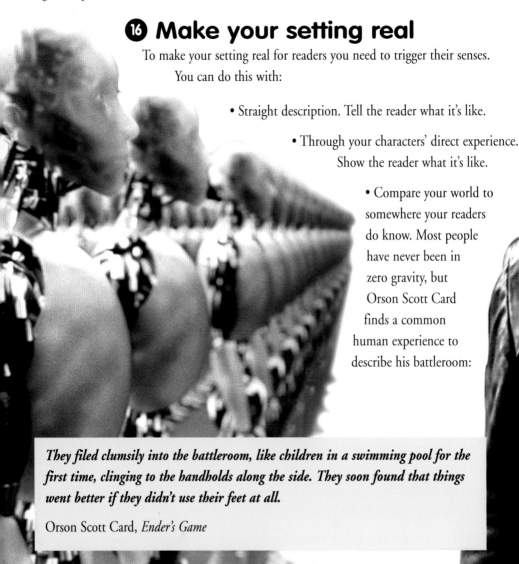

To make your setting real for readers you need to trigger their senses. You can do this with:

• Straight description. Tell the reader what it's like.

• Through your characters' direct experience. Show the reader what it's like.

• Compare your world to somewhere your readers do know. Most people have never been in zero gravity, but Orson Scott Card finds a common human experience to describe his battleroom:

> *They filed clumsily into the battleroom, like children in a swimming pool for the first time, clinging to the handholds along the side. They soon found that things went better if they didn't use their feet at all.*
>
> Orson Scott Card, *Ender's Game*

⑰ Define the threat

Whatever is threatening your world, it will affect the way you describe your setting. Look again at the opening of the Arthur C. Clarke story on page 19. See how it tells you where you are and combines action (travelling through space) with an instant sense of foreboding: 'the shadow that lay across civilization'.

TIPS AND TECHNIQUES

A key storytelling skill is to say just enough to move the story forward, while hinting that there is much more still to find out. If your world needs a lot of explaining, try putting the main details in a prologue. Write it from the perspective of one of your characters.

Now it's your turn

A dramatic opening

Write an opening story scene of about 200 words. Take ten minutes. Combine setting details with some piece of action – maybe your hero arriving. Try adding a hint of doom too. Choose the most descriptive verbs you can think of. For example, a starship doesn't just fly, it speeds through space; a power-plant throbs with pent-up energy; a red sun looms through the solar dust.

⑱ Picking details

Once you know your world really well, pick out only the most striking things to describe. Think brief. Think sharp. Think exciting. From the start, give them vivid clues to trigger their senses. Have something happening at the same time – something mysterious that snags the reader's curiosity.

⑲ Good setting recipe 1

Combine description with action:

> *Among the trees something was happening that was not meant for human eyes … a shaft of blue light cut the darkness. It came from a narrow opening in a high tooth-shaped rock, and within the opening was a pair of iron gates thrown wide, and beyond them a tunnel. Shadows moved on the trees as a strange procession entered through the gates and down into the hill. They were a small people.*
>
> Alan Garner, *The Moon of Gomrath*

⑳ Good setting recipe 2

Combine description with action from a character's point of view:

> *Holly rolled off her futon and stumbled into the shower. That was one advantage of living near the earth's core – the water was always hot. No natural light, of course, but that was a small price to pay for privacy. Underground. The last human-free zone. There was nothing like coming home from a long day on the job, switching off your shield and sinking into a bubbling slime pool. Bliss.*
>
> Eoin Colfer (left), *Artemis Fowl*

Now it's your turn

A striking opening

Write the opening paragraph to your story, and see how you can mix setting descriptions with action. Choose words that fizz – instead of your character walking make him flee, fly or speed through the Grim Gorge. Think of striking images, like Alan Garner's tooth-shaped rock which creates a very sinister atmosphere. Think of using telling adjectives too. Sparkling is stronger than shiny – sparkling does; shiny just is.

㉑ Good setting recipe 3

Combine description with action from a character's point of view and make them hurry:

Holly grabbed the remains of a nettle smoothie from the cooler and drank it in the tunnels. As usual there was chaos in the main thoroughfare. Airborne sprites jammed the avenue like stones in a bottle. The gnomes weren't helping either, lumbering along with their big swinging behinds blocking two lanes. Swear toads infested every damp patch, cursing like sailors.

Eoin Colfer, *Artemis Fowl*

㉒ Good setting recipe 4

If your fantasy world needs a lot of explanation, set the scene in the first chapter and you won't have to use so much description later on. This device is employed by C. S. Lewis:

This must be a simply enormous wardrobe! thought Lucy ... Then she noticed that there was something crunching under her feet ... But instead of feeling the hard, smooth wood of the floor of the wardrobe she felt something soft and powdery and extremely cold ... Lucy felt a little frightened but she felt very inquisitive and excited too.

C. S. Lewis, *The Lion, The Witch and the Wardrobe*

CHAPTER 3: CREATING CHARACTERS

HEROES

The key to successful stories is devising believable heroes, villains and a valuable supporting cast. The main thing when creating a hero, such as King Arthur (right), is that you must care deeply about them, otherwise you won't be able to make the readers care about them.

❶ Finding a hero's name

Philip Pullman says Lyra from *Northern Lights* stepped into his mind fully formed, name and all. J. K. Rowling collects words she likes the sound of. Dumbledore means bumblebee in Old English. If you're stuck, flick through a baby names book, an atlas index or telephone book. If you make a name up, say it out loud to see what it sounds like.

TIPS AND TECHNIQUES

Start a 'special words' list in your notebook. Write down any word that catches your imagination. You'll know where to look the next time you are stuck for a name. Don't make it too complicated for readers to remember. Simple names like Kit, Gem or Will can often be more memorable.

❷ Build up a picture

You need to know what your hero looks like. Think about their clothes, their hair, height and build, what they like and don't like. Are they good at something? What are their weaknesses? Think how their weaknesses might play a part in your story. For instance, Lyra is a liar. She also lacks imagination, but both of these flaws often help her out of tough situations.

Now it's your turn

Know your hero

Your hero needs a past. Brainstorm everything you can think of in five minutes – who they are, where they live, whether they have a family, go to work or school. Here is Eoin Colfer's brief history of Holly Short (right) in *Artemis Fowl*:

Technically she was an elf, fairy being a general term. She was a leprechaun too, but that was just a job … Cupid was her great-grandfather. Her mother was a European elf with a fiery temper and a willowy frame.

❸ Give strengths and weaknesses

No one wants to read stories about people with perfect lives. Heroes need serious personal problems as well as some major external threat to overcome. In Louise Lawrence's *Dreamweaver*, Eth's major personal problem revolves round her cruel brother Liadd, but this story also weaves into a wider threat: her planet is about to be colonized by greedy Earth settlers. Her strengths and weaknesses are played out between these two predicaments, adding drama and suspense.

❹ Choose heroic qualities

Imagine meeting your hero. You like something about them straight away and you want to be friends. What do you especially admire? Find out as much as possible before you start your story. Something in their past may set the mystery in motion.

❺ Get inspiration from others

Base them on a classic hero but don't simply copy them. That would be plagiarism. Take some characteristics, adapt them and mix them with real people or other characters. For example, if you mixed a bit of Sherlock Holmes with a class swot you might end up with a character like Hermione (right) in the *Harry Potter* books.

Now it's your turn

In their shoes

For ten minutes put on your hero's shoes. Think about their weaknesses – perhaps a wild imagination or a hot temper. Think of their good points too – a sense of humour, a caring nature or standing up for others. These could get them into trouble too.

TIPS AND TECHNIQUES

Pretend you are your hero. Write their diary.

❻ Create a clear profile

Describe your hero near the start of your story so readers don't set off imagining someone being tall and dark, and you later reveal them to be red-haired and weedy. You'll risk losing readers' good will. Your hero also needs a history. Make it brief, but make sure you remember it as you write the story.

❼ What's the problem?

In *Dovey Coe* by Frances O'Roark Dowell, Dovey is so likeable, it is hard to understand how she has been charged with murder. However, she does speak her mind, often in scathing terms. She also sets out to make a very public enemy of Parnell Caraway: 'I'd just as soon shoot him as look at him …' she says. Later, this is used as evidence. But she tells us herself, 'I admit that's my biggest drawback, not thinking things through far enough.'

Now it's your turn

On the record

Open a file on your hero. Make out an official report, which you can add to later as more ideas come to you. Begin by filling out their personal details: name, age, address, nationality, previous addresses, details of immediate relatives. Describe the hero's appearance, and any identifying characteristics. Give details of how they live and what they do. Do some sketches too, or cut out faces from magazines and newspapers.

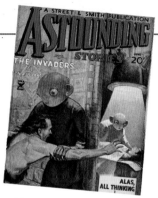

❽ What type of villain?

In science fiction your hero's main external enemy is likely to be some physical disaster, but you also need some enemy characters too. They might be evil like Darth Vader, or their wickedness might not be so easy to spot.

❾ The face of evil

First think about what makes your villains so evil. Are they hungry for power? Do they want great wealth or some special knowledge that will help them control everyone, or make them immortal? Are they simply cruel and get their pleasure from destroying things? Are they envious of your hero? Did they start off good and then turn to evil ways?

Now it's your turn

Know your villain

In a ten-minute practice, brainstorm your chief villain. What is his or her motivation? Think about his or her weaknesses too and how these might help the story. Repeat the exercise on page 36 with your baddie as your focus.

TIPS AND TECHNIQUES

The more you question your villains, the more you'll find out about them, and the more intriguing they'll become. Sometimes the most evil thing is something you can't quite see. The writer can reveal it indirectly through the fear in other characters' minds.

Literary villains

Long John Silver

Long John Silver seems
like a goodie when
Jim Hawkins first
sees him at the Spy-Glass Tavern:

*His left leg was cut off close by the hip, and
under his left shoulder he carried a crutch,
which he managed with wonderful
dexterity, hopping upon it like a bird. He
was tall and strong, with a face as big as
a ham – plain and pale, but intelligent
and smiling.*

Robert Louis Stevenson, *Treasure Island*

Bartholome the Brazilian

In *Pirates!*, Bartholome is a buccaneer
turned Jamaican plantation owner.
When Nancy Kington meets him at her
father's funeral, we know at once that
he will become a serious threat
to her:

*He took my hand. His long fingers were
heavy with rings, square-cut rubies and
emeralds. He stood looking down at me
with eyes so black as to show no pupil.
They held a gleam of red, almost purple, like
overripe cherries, or deadly nightshade berries.*

Celia Rees, *Pirates!*

Gagool

Gagool is the aged witchdoctor in
service to wicked King Twala. She
is set to kill Allan Quartermain and
his friends:

*Nearer and nearer waltzed Gagool looking
for the world like an animated crooked
stick or comma, her horrid eyes gleaming
and glowing with a most unholy lustre.*

H. Rider Haggard, *King Solomon's Mines*

TIPS AND TECHNIQUES

*Villains will have weaknesses. In The Mummy, Benny's greed leaves him trapped forever in the
City of the Dead. But don't forget: sometimes villains have good points too!*

⑩ The rest of the cast

As in real life, your heroes will be judged by the company they keep. Scenes between your hero and friends are a good way to show the reader what he or she is really like as a person. How would we know how loyal Harry Potter is without seeing him with his friends (left)?

⑪ Goodies vs baddies

You will need 'goodies' and 'baddies' to help or harm your hero. In the brainstorming exercise on page 21, you dealt yourself a hero's helper and a villain's henchman. Can you now develop these ideas? Make up your own beings, or adapt some from a host of marvellous fantasy creatures in myths and fairy tales. What about a villain such as Gollum (right) in the *Lord of the Rings* trilogy, or a winged horse like Pegasus who might whisk your hero to safety, or some variation on the snake-headed Medusa from Greek myth, who could turn a person to stone just by looking at them?

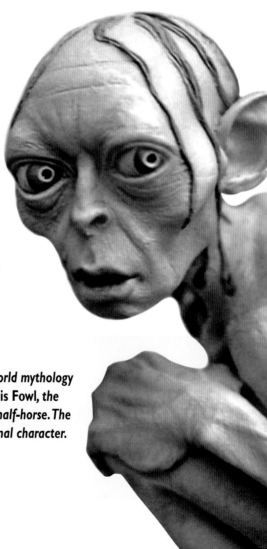

TIPS AND TECHNIQUES

For extraordinary creatures find a dictionary of world mythology in the library. See what you can recycle. In Artemis Fowl, the fairyland security expert is a centaur – half-man, half-horse. The mix of old with new can make a wonderfully original character.

Now it's your turn

CETUS

ARGUS

SPHINX

MEDUSA

Picture your characters

In your next practice, try sketching your characters. Ask your creations what special powers they have and how these will make your story more exciting. Hunt for good names that tell the reader something about the characters. Remember that your characters each need some special quality or flaw that will make them instantly more marvellous or dastardly.

⑫ The mark of a character

In *The Lord of the Rings*, Frodo seems an unlikely hero to take on the impossible quest against the mighty Sauron. One way that Tolkien makes us think that Froddo has hidden qualitiesis by showing us his friend Sam's unshakeable devotion to him.

⑬ Creature concoction

A creature from Greek mythology has the hind parts of a dragon, the body of a goat, the forelegs of a lion and the head of each. Mixed in equal proportions, and abracadabra! – you have a Chimera (above). Can you come up with any scary creature combinations? *Tyrannosaurus Rex* meets Giant Vampire Bat meets … ?

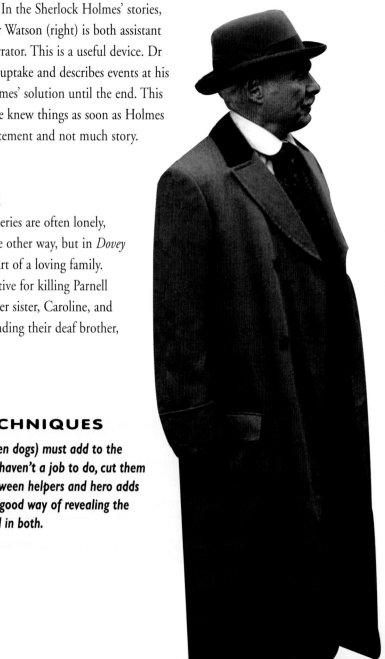

⑭ Standing out

Minor characters won't be as developed as your hero and villain, but they must still seem 'real'. A good way to bring them to life is to give them one or two obvious characteristics – like Mahbub Ali's bright-red beard in Rudyard Kipling's *Kim*.

⑮ Read famous examples

In the Sherlock Holmes' stories, Dr Watson (right) is both assistant and narrator. This is a useful device. Dr Watson is often slow on the uptake and describes events at his own pace, not revealing Holmes' solution until the end. This way he builds suspense. If we knew things as soon as Holmes did, there would be less excitement and not much story.

⑯ Build up relationships

The main characters in mysteries are often lonely, orphaned or isolated in some other way, but in *Dovey Coe*, the heroine Dovey is part of a loving family. This gives her a possible motive for killing Parnell because he wants to marry her sister, Caroline, and makes dark threats about sending their deaf brother, Amos, to an institution.

TIPS AND TECHNIQUES

Supporting characters (even dogs) must add to the story in some way. If they haven't a job to do, cut them out. The conversations between helpers and hero adds variety, interest and are a good way of revealing the thought processes involved in both.

Now it's your turn

Writing biographies

Choose five people who you know really well. They could be friends of the family or classmates. Make each one as fascinating as possible in no more than three sentences each.

⓱ Memorable characters

You will not go into as much depth with your supporting characters as your hero, so you must find ways to fix them in your readers' minds. Be quick and interesting so they add to the story, not hold it up. Here we meet Herod Sayle's trusty assistant, Mr Grin, for the first time in *Stormbreaker*:

> *From a distance it looked as if he was smiling, but as he grew closer Alex gasped. The man had two horrendous scars, one on each side of his mouth, twisting all the way up to his ears. It was as if someone had attempted to cut his face in half.*

Anthony Horowitz, *Stormbreaker*

⓲ Animals

Of course, your assistants may not all be human. You could include animals. The fifth member of Enid Blyton's *Famous Five* sleuthing team is a dog called Timmy.

WHO'S SPEAKING?

Before you start to write your story, you must decide whose point of view you want to show. Will you write from your hero's point of view, or do you want to describe everything that happens to all your characters? Do you want to write from the third person or first person perspective? The choice is yours ...

❶ The omniscient

Traditional tales use the omniscient, or all-knowing, viewpoint. This way of writing tells readers all that is going on in a scene in a rather detached way, like a film-maker shooting a movie. The example below from Jack London's *White Fang* shows the use of this way of writing:

A second cry arose, piercing the silence with needle-like shrillness. Both men located the sound. It was to the rear, somewhere in the snow expanse they had just traversed. A third and answering cry arose, also to the rear and to the left of the second cry.

'They're after us, Bill,' said the man at the front. His voice sounded hoarse and unreal, and he had spoken with apparent effort.

'Meat is scarce,' answered his comrade. 'I ain't seen a rabbit sign for days.'

Jack London, *White Fang*

❷ The third person

Writing from only one character's point of view is called the third-person viewpoint. It is usually written in the past tense. It takes us right inside the character's head and involves us more closely. For example, the Jack London extract might go like this:

Bill's heart leapt. A second cry! It pierced the silence with needle-like shrillness. He swung around to locate it. It's behind us, he thought, back on our trail.

Then from the front of the sled he heard Henry mutter, his voice hoarse, 'They're after us, Bill.'

Bill grunted, struggling to hide his own fear. 'Meat is scarce,' he said. 'I ain't seen a rabbit sign for days.'

❸ The first person

The first-person viewpoint, that is 'I/we', is closest to the spoken word. It is intimate and exciting. Your characters will be revealing their innermost thoughts. You can use straight narrative, letters, emails or diary entries. The disadvantage is that you can only reveal other characters' views when recording their speech in dialogue or reporting on their behaviour.

Now it's your turn

Good vs evil

Take 30 minutes to write a short action scene between your hero and villain. First write it from the omniscient or all-knowing viewpoint. Next write it from your hero's viewpoint and then from the villain's. Experiment with the first person and the present tense too. Read your efforts aloud to yourself. Which version do you prefer and why?

READY TO WRITE

When your story begins to take shape in your mind, sum up the main theme and plot in a few paragraphs. This is called a synopsis. It will help you keep your story on track. Tell just enough to be intriguing but don't give away the end.

❶ Back cover inspiration

On the back covers of books, the 'blurb' briefly sets the scene and makes readers want to find out more. A synopsis should do the same. Here is an extract from a blurb:

Tom and his friend Ann find life a bit too exciting when they are caught up in the bloodshed and mayhem of the wars between England and France that scarred the 14th century. Tom is kidnapped, falls off a palace, down a well and in love – oh, and he makes a total mess of the Pope's dinner.

Terry Jones, *The Lady and the Squire*

Now it's your turn

Hungry readers

Sum up your story in a single striking sentence, then develop it in two or three short paragraphs. Try to whet your readers' appetites. Show where your story is going without giving away the actual ending.

❷ Create a synopsis

Before they start writing their stories, novelists often list all their chapters outlining what will happen in each one. This is called a chapter synopsis. Once you have worked out the main scenes, you could also develop each one into a separate chapter and so create a novel.

❸ Make a story map

Now you have a synopsis that says what your story is about, a cast of characters, a setting, and you know from whose viewpoint you wish to tell the tale. This combines to create a story map.

❹ Split into scenes

Before film-makers can start filming, they must know the main story episodes and decide how they can best tell their story in filmed images. To help them, they map out the plot (the sequence of events) in a series of sketches called storyboards. You can do this for your story. Draw the main episodes in pictures. Add a few notes that say what is happening in each scene.

TIPS AND TECHNIQUES

Writing a synopsis can bring unexpected ideas to the surface. If you can't describe your story in a couple of paragraphs, it is too complicated. Simplify it.

❺ Get inspiration from a classic

Here are some storyboard captions for Sherlock Holmes' *The Adventure of the Speckled Band* by Sir Arthur Conan Doyle:

1. Helen Stoner arrives at Holmes' rooms, saying she's afraid for her life.

2. Tells Holmes about the mysterious death of her twin sister and her dying words about a speckled band.

3. Gives some family history and tells of her violent stepfather Dr Roylott who controls the money left her by her mother.

4. After she leaves, Dr Roylott bursts in and threatens Holmes if he starts interfering.

5. Holmes and Watson travel to Stoke Moran, Roylott's home, to investigate; they discover several strange features in the dead sister's room.

6. Later they go secretly to spend the night in the room, and Holmes warns Watson of the grave danger.

7. In the night, Holmes raises the alarm, lashing out with his cane.

8. A scream comes from Dr Roylott's room. They find him dead with a speckled band round his head.

9. Holmes explains the case to Watson.

TIPS AND TECHNIQUES

Don't let a novel's length put you off from starting one. If you use the story map approach it is often easier to write a novel than it is to write a good short story.

❻ Write a novel?

Novels have beginnings, middles and ends just like short stories, but the stories themselves are more complex. They have more details, more character development and subplots. The chapters make the storytelling manageable. Each one has a beginning, middle and end, like a mini-story inside the larger one, but it also carries the story forward, adding more mystery and creating more and more suspense.

To turn the short story *The Adventure of the Speckled Band* into a novel, look at each scene caption and think how to make it into an episode that shows readers more about the characters and their problems. Chapter 1 could start with Helen Stoner waking in terror, then travelling to London to seek help. You could show all the difficulties she has leaving the house secretly. A novel, then, is not a short story made longer, but a short story made fatter. The suspense is built up from chapter to chapter, and any mysteries spun out so that readers are drawn more deeply into the story.

Now it's your turn

Weave a story web

If you're still struggling to come up with a plot for your story, get a large piece of paper. In the centre draw a rough sketch of your hero. Put them inside a circle. As you are drawing, imagine that you are that hero, looking outside the circle, trying to solve a riddle. Then draw six spokes from your hero circle. Each spoke leads to an empty circle. In one minute, without thinking at all, write in each circle one thing that you have discovered. It can be an object or a piece of information – the dog didn't bark; all the doors and windows were locked at the crime scene; a torn up plane ticket … The wilder your thoughts, the more likely they will lead to something you can use.

❼ Great beginnings

You have planned your plot and are ready to start your story. Focus on your hero. Put on your hero's skin. Become your hero. Think about 'your' problems. What is at stake? Where will you start the story?

❽ Hook your readers

Some stories leap straight into a dramatic scene, then backtrack shortly afterwards to explain things to readers. Others start with a prologue, giving the historical context. You could start with a brief scene set just before a crisis comes. This lets you show the hero's usual life just before a conflict makes it worse (the Viking invasions, for example). Your hero must then take action or face the consequences.

❾ Bizarre beginnings

In *The Lady and the Squire*, Terry Jones uses some most unexpected comparisons to help us sympathize with hero Tom. The writer speaks directly to the reader about the characters:

> *If you've ever sat astride a man-eating shark and dangled bits of raw flesh in front of it as the creature starts to plunge down into the dark abyss of the sea, taking you with it, you'll have a pretty good idea of how Tom felt in his new job as squire to Henry, Duke of Lancaster. For the time being, Tom was keeping his head above water, but he knew that, at any moment, the Duke might eat him for lunch.*

Terry Jones, *The Lady and the Squire*

⑩ Tense starts

V. A. Richardson's *The House of Windjammer* starts with a shipwreck and the loss of a family fortune. From the first lines, we know things will only get worse for the family:

> *They were lost. All aboard the Sirius knew it now. Lucien Windjammer cursed under his breath. The Sirius rode uneasily on the swell, moving through the fog like a ghost ship.*
>
> V. A. Richardson, *The House of Windjammer*

TIPS AND TECHNIQUES

Study lots of opening sentences. Decide which ones work best and why. Make your own opening mysterious or dramatic or funny. Write it and rewrite it. Introduce the conflict at once, or soon afterwards. Send your heroes on their way.

⓫ Set the tone

For good beginnings, create suspense, make the hero engaging and set the tone, whether it's dramatic, spooky, humorous or chilling. Here are two examples:

'My name is Dovey Coe, and I reckon it don't matter if you like me or not. I'm here to lay the record straight, to let you know them folks saying I done terrible things are liars. I aim to prove it, too. I hated Parnell Caraway as much as the next person, but I didn't kill him.'

Frances O'Roark Dowell, *Dovey Coe*

The boy crept up to the fence and looked around. There was the familiar sign ... KEEP OUT! PRIVATE PROPERTY. TRESPASSERS WILL BE SHOT. And hanging next to it, just to make sure that the message was clearly understood, were the bodies of several dead animals. Strung up like criminals, wire twisted round their broken necks.

Charlie Higson, *SilverFin*

TIPS AND TECHNIQUES

To learn how to write smack-in-the-eye first sentences, go to the library and read as many examples as possible. Make a note of your favourites. Story beginnings introduce the hero and their problems and make the reader want to know what happens next.

Draw the readers in by:

Creating mystery

Hassan. Where was he?

The question burned in Kibi's mind as he slammed the house door behind him and stepped into the village lane. It was a week or more since Kibi had last seen him.

Whenever he passed Hassan's house on the edge of the square it seemed shut up and sad.

Tish Farrell, *Sea Running*

Making characters intriguing

I write for many reasons.

I write, not least to quiet my grief. I find that by reliving the adventures that I shared with Minerva, I can lessen the pain of our parting. I must find new diversions that fit my station now that I have put up my pistols and cutlass and have exchanged my breeches for a dress.

Celia Rees, *Pirates!*

Being funny

The Queen looked out across the Mudfords' living room and wished everyone a happy Christmas. Colin scowled. Easy for you, he thought. Bet you got what you wanted. Bet if you wanted a microscope you got a microscope. Bet your tree was covered with microscopes. Bet nobody gave you daggy school shoes for Christmas.

Morris Gleitzman,
Two Weeks with the Queen

Being dramatic

I disappeared on the night before my twelfth birthday. July 28 1988. Only now can I at last tell the whole extraordinary story, the true story. Kensuke made me promise that I would say nothing, nothing at all, until at least ten years had passed.

Michael Morpurgo, *Kensuke's Kingdom*

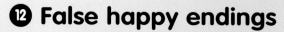

⑫ False happy endings

If story beginnings must grip, then middles should grip harder. From the first page the story needs to build tension and suspense. If your story is drifting then try to see things through your characters' eyes. One good ploy to create suspense is to have a false happy ending. For example, the hero seems to have saved the world from invasion, but just when everyone is celebrating, a more deadly alien force appears on the planet's scanners. This gives the writer the chance to build up the excitement on an even bigger scale.

⑬ Maintain the action

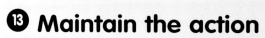

Plenty of activity also holds readers' interest. Keep your characters engaged with their quest at all times, on the move, working things out, coming to the wrong conclusions, having fights, escaping disasters.

⑭ Give your heroes problems

If your heroes are time-challenged this instantly adds drama. Will Ender be trained in time to destroy the next alien fleet (Orson Scott Card's *Ender's Game*)? Will Eth learn what she must before the unwanted spacecraft lands on her planet (*Dreamweaver*)? Will Lina and Doon solve the problems of their dying city before the lights go out forever (*The City of Ember*)?

Now it's your turn

There's strength in weakness

Focus on your hero's flaws or weaknesses. In five minutes write your first thoughts on how these might complicate and add drama to your story. Do the same for any other main characters. Perhaps your hero's friend turns out to have doubtful motives. Think how these factors might bring your story to a climax. Try the whole exercise again, but write with your non-writing hand. See what crops up …

⓯ Challenge your reader

Don't forget to stir and complicate and pile on the challenges. If your hero has been pursued by some bully or aggressor, make the reader think they have found a new target … then let the villain return with some worse torment. This time your hero must deal with this situation once and for all. How they decide to do this, and whether it will work, adds some new suspense. Your hero's weaknesses could come to the fore too.

TIPS AND TECHNIQUES

Action scenes should spring from the characters' own plans, not from your need to revive a flagging story. But when you do include them, make them as exciting as possible. Your characters' weaknesses can add more twists and turns to the story.

16 Increase the tension

It's all too easy for a story to sag after a good opening. Now is the time to turn up the tension. Think of your hero's problems. How can you make them worse? Stir and complicate!

TIPS AND TECHNIQUES

If story middles seem 'thin', pile on the challenges for your hero; make their lives a real misery! If you run out of ideas, look through your research notes.

17 Add more threats

In *The Edge* by Alan Gibbons, Danny and Cathy escape from Chris Kane and find refuge with Danny's grandparents. But Chris Kane sets out to track them down, and Danny's grandfather has a racist dislike of Danny. And finally, there are the racist bullies at Danny's new school. All these threats intertwine and build towards a nail-biting climax.

Now it's your turn

Problems escalator ...

Brainstorm your main character's problems AGAIN! First write their flaws or weaknesses at the top of the page. In the bottom left-hand corner start drawing a staircase. The bottom step will be your hero's problem at the story's start. Write it on the step. Draw a second step and write the next problem on it (make it a little bit worse). Repeat the process up the page for as long as you can. Keep glancing at your hero's flaws and weaknesses. Give yourself two minutes for each step and write only your first thoughts.

18 Add in the time factor

In *Walk Two Moons* by Sharon Creech, Salamanca goes on a car trip with her grandparents. They only have a week for their journey across America and mean to visit all the places that Salamanca's mother stopped at on an earlier trip. Salamanca is desperate to reach her mother's final destination in time for her birthday. On the last lap Grandma is bitten by a snake. Will they reach Lewiston in time?

TIPS AND TECHNIQUES

Fatten story middles by asking your hero 'How could things get worse for you?' then make it happen. Place obstacles in their path. Have them make the wrong choices. Let them make mistakes.

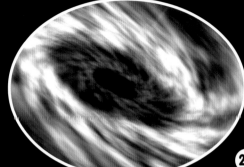

⑲ Choose an ending

Finding a good ending is perhaps the hardest part of storytelling. Some writers like to think up their exact ending before they start writing. Others don't want to know until they get there.

⑳ Wrapping up endings

As you plan your ending, think again about problems, conflict and resolution. Good endings must bring the hero's problems and conflicts (plot) to a climax, and then resolve them in satisfying ways. The ending should also refer in some way to the story's beginning and thus remind readers that something important has changed in the course of the story, e.g. the hero has overcome some weakness.

㉑ Create an intriguing finish

Most readers like some sort of happy ending, but don't be predictable.

In science fiction the endings may involve mixed feelings. Your heroes might have overcome some enemy and learned or gained something, but they may also have lost something, or had to make some sacrifices. So rather than a 'happy' end, make it hopeful instead. In *Star Wars*, when Luke Skywalker refuses to be lured to the dark side, Emperor Palpatine turns all his evil against him. Seeing his son being destroyed, Darth Vader destroys Palpatine but is wounded himself. Before he dies he asks Luke to remove the mask. He dies as Anakin Skywalker and not the monster he had become. For Luke this ending is desperately hard, gaining and losing his father all at once, but the forces of good have been saved.

Choose your own ending

Read the ending of your favourite story. Can you think of an alternative ending? See if you can write it, then put it aside. Go back and read both versions later. Now which ending do you prefer and why?

㉒ Add a twist

Many Sci-Fi stories have twist-in-the-tale endings. All along you've been assuming your enemy is in a different country, only to find out they are in the same room as you. To do this successfully, you need to drop subtle clues throughout your story. This is called foreshadowing. The reader will be surprised by the twist, but will then think, 'I should have realized!'

Bad endings are those that:

• Fizzle out because you've run out of ideas;

• Rely on some coincidence or surprise twist that hasn't been mentioned in the story;

• Fail to show how the characters have changed in some way;

• Are too grim and depressing and leave the reader with no hope.

TIPS AND TECHNIQUES

Don't forget to look at your story map if you are stuck. Or brainstorm your hero in a circle again from page 49.

㉓ Dramatic climaxes

In the last part of your story, the hero's problems must reach a dramatic climax. After this the hero's problems will be solved, or at least changed for the better. Happy-ever-after endings should be avoided in realistic fiction. Instead, aim for an upbeat ending, where things work out hopefully rather than perfectly.

㉔ New beginnings

At the start of *The Edge*, Danny and Cathy escape by train from London to his grandparents' gloomy northern town. Danny has serious doubts that it is the promised land. But at the end of the book, when he repeats the journey and all his conflicts have been resolved, he has a different view:

He imagines the lowering mass of the Edge approaching through the late afternoon and feels a rush of exhilaration as powerful as in the last fifty metres of a race. He's looking forward to it, to freedom, to the promised land.

Alan Gibbons,
The Edge

㉕ Heartwarming endings

At the end of Jack London's *White Fang*, the wolf has recovered from his wounds and meets Collie's puppies – his own offspring:

The other puppies came sprawling toward him, to Collie's great disgust; and he gravely permitted them to clamber and tumble over him … and he lay with half-shut, patient eyes drowsing in the sun.

Jack London, *White Fang*

TIPS AND TECHNIQUES

Good stories may seem to go in straight lines, beginning, middle and end, but they also go round in circles. The hero returns to the place where they started, but they are wiser now.

CHAPTER 6: WINNING WORDS

MAKING WORDS WORK

Words are valuable things. Every one you use should work the hardest it can for your story. Readers can access your thrilling story so much more powerfully if it is free from rambling sentences and too many adjectives.

❶ Use vivid imagery

If you can sum up scenes in images that trigger the senses, it is like adding special effects to your story. Try using metaphors and similes to bring your story to life. These are word pictures. A metaphor is when you call a man a mouse, meaning that he is scared; a simile is a comparison: as quiet as a mouse. Choose striking verbs too.

In the *Dinosaur Summer* example below, one-syllable verbs like 'dropped' and 'thrust' are good action words that echo the activity. The 'truckload of knives' is a stunning simile. It knocks the breath out of you.

> *And the death eagle dropped on her like a truckload of knives. Its white-gorgeted griffin's head thrust again and again, beak stripping skin into ribbons, shredding tendons.*
>
> Greg Bear, *Dinosaur Summer*

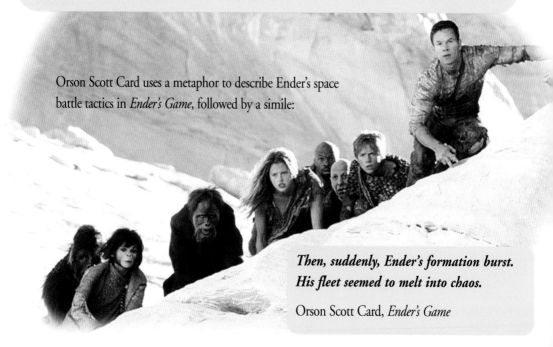

Orson Scott Card uses a metaphor to describe Ender's space battle tactics in *Ender's Game*, followed by a simile:

> *Then, suddenly, Ender's formation burst. His fleet seemed to melt into chaos.*
>
> Orson Scott Card, *Ender's Game*

❷ Change the rhythm and length of your sentences

This is another way to keep readers reading. Like the *Dinosaur Summer* example, action scenes need short, sharp phrases that focus exactly on what is happening. But if you are building up for something scary, spin out the phrases a little, add some sharp details that make the scene more real. Imagine yourself creeping up on your reader … Then strike!

❸ Change the mood

Changes in mood will also give your story edge. Fiction often deals with catastrophes, but if you are gloomy from start to finish, no one will want to read about it. In a tension-mounting scene some humour can give readers light relief. Or if your story is humorous, then try to give it some serious angles too. In the same way, readers also need a break from action sequences. This lets your readers catch their breath and allows the dust to settle before the story moves on. By breaking up the mood in this way, your story will work more effectively.

Now it's your turn

Using words effectively

To make your writing bite, exercise your word-making skills. Brainstorm more lists: How many words for 'flying' can you think of? How many words for 'shine'? Reinvent sayings, for example, the cliché 'As white as snow' could become 'As white as … a snow goose's tail, or a snowdrop, or an Alaskan snowdrift'. Read the dictionary. Play word games.

TIPS AND TECHNIQUES

Remember that your characters will have different moods too. Use them. Try ending a dramatic scene on a cliffhanger. Leave your heroes in peril and drive your readers to find out what happens next.

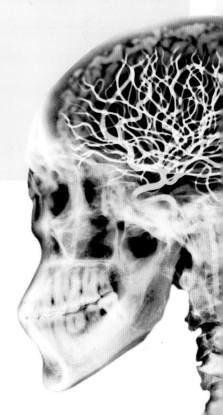

❹ Use sharp focus

Keep descriptive passages short. Think of snapshot images. If possible make your description reveal something about the characters. In this example from *Walk Two Moons*, Sharon Creech shows us Salamanca's deep sense of loss:

> *Just over a year ago, my father plucked me up like a weed and took me and all our belongings (no, that is not true – he did not bring the chestnut tree or the willow or the maple or the hayloft …)*

Sharon Creech, *Walk Two Moons*

❺ Write with bite

When writing action scenes, choose words that 'sound' most like the action you are describing – 'smash' is more powerful than 'hit'; 'shriek' is more piercing than 'cry'. Vary the length of your sentences, too. Try short ones for fast actions and longer ones for more lingering events.

> *Sssssssssssssssssssss.*
> *Colin watched as the air hissed out of the tyre of the Mercedes … How dare they drive cars with automatic aerials and dual anti-lock braking systems and wipers on the headlamps when they couldn't even cure cancer?*

Morris Gleitzman, *Two Weeks with the Queen*

Now it's your turn

Try some word play

Cut up scrap paper into at least 60 small squares. Brainstorm or pick out 30 adjectives and 30 nouns at random from any book. Write one word on each square and keep the nouns and adjectives separate. Then keep dealing yourself one from each pile. See what pairs you get: a blue-eyed boulder, a silken shield, a frozen feather.

❻ Paint pictures with words

Another way to quickly bring scenes alive for readers is to use imagery. In *Dovey Coe*, Dovey describes a scene in winter: "Now the trees … stand dusted in white, and it looks like they got ghosts dancing through their branches." Imagine your scene in detail and then pick out the most telling details to vividly paint the scene.

TIPS AND TECHNIQUES

Increase suspense by building to an exciting moment: give readers hints of the danger to come and then pounce.

❼ Crank up the suspense and drama

Foreshadowing is an essential tool in all fiction writing. It means dropping hints about coming events. In the *Harry Potter* books, remarks about the fate of Harry's family are used to remind us of Voldemort, sometimes with just a hint of worry, sometimes to stir up some real fear. And whenever Harry's scar starts throbbing, we know Voldemort is on the prowl.

> *It was a unicorn all right, and it was dead ... Harry had taken one step towards it when a slithering sound made him freeze where he stood. A bush on the edge of the clearing quivered ... Then out of the shadows, a hooded figure came crawling like some stalking beast ...*

J. K. Rowling, *Harry Potter and the Philosopher's Stone*

❽ Use dramatic irony

Dramatic irony is another useful device. This is where the reader knows something important that the characters don't know. In *A Series of Unfortunate Events* (right), Lemony Snicket uses dramatic irony in all his stories – forewarning us of the horrible things that are going to happen, just when the characters are having a moment's happiness.

❾ Heighten the action

Action scenes need crisp phrases that focus on what is happening. In *The Edge*, Danny and his mother escape from Chris Kane's flat. Notice the use of the present tense. What do you think it adds to the scene?

> *'Go!' says Mum. 'We've got to go … now!'*
>
> *It's like the floor is tilting, the wall's closing in. Everything distorts … This is Chris's world, the terror zone. But there is no way back. They're running down the first flight of stairs. As they turn to descend to the ground floor they hear Chris's voice from the flat.*
>
> *'Cath! Cathy!'*
>
> Alan Gibbons, *The Edge*

TIPS AND TECHNIQUES

Action scenes should stick to the action and should not be too drawn out. Use short, punchy phrases and limit description to the bare minimum.

Now it's your turn

True words

Pick a word from one of your favourite books and see how many words of a similar meaning you can think of. You could also pick a new word from the dictionary every day to improve your word power. Find ways to use it – make a poem or limerick.

CREATING DIALOGUE

Dialogue lets readers 'hear' what your characters have to say in their own words. If well written, it brings them to life. Conversations between characters are also a good way to give information that pushes the story forward.

❶ The art of eavesdropping

The best way to learn how people talk is to eavesdrop. But don't simply listen for snippets of gossip. Pay attention to the actual words used. Tune in to conversations over lunch, in the street or on the bus. Look out for interesting expressions or particular patterns of speech. Watch people's body language, too. What do they do when they're telling someone a secret they promised to keep?

Now it's your turn

Breaking bad news

Your best friend urgently needs you but your parents say you can't go out. Write the conversation as you break the news to your friend. Do you end up falling out? Don't rely on tags like 'yelled' or 'cried' to show the mood. Now revise it and take out any unnecessary 'saids'. Cut down the words to the bare bones. This is the essential skill of editing your own work!

❷ Following convention

The way dialogue is written follows certain conventions or rules. It is usual to start a new paragraph for every new speaker. What they say is enclosed in single or double inverted commas, followed by speech tags, e.g. 'he said/she said', to indicate the speaker. Speech tags may be left out if we know who is speaking, or placed in the middle of some speech lines to give the impression of the pauses in real conversation.

The extract on the right is taken from *Dinosaur Summer*, by Greg Bear. The author begins a new paragraph for each new speaker, making the extract easy for the reader to follow.

'I have a confession to make.'

Peter narrowed his eyes. 'What sort of confession?'

'I got a telegram from your mother. Last week. I didn't bother to tell you.'

'Why?' Peter asked.

'It was addressed to me.' Anthony returned to the front room and pulled the crumpled piece of paper from his shirt pocket. 'She's worried about you. Summer's here. She thinks you're going to catch polio from all these crowds. She forbids you to swim in municipal pools.'

Peter had hoped his mother might have sent a message inviting him to come to Chicago for a visit. 'Oh,' he said.

Greg Bear, *Dinosaur Summer*

TIPS AND TECHNIQUES

Dialogue gives the impression of real speech; it doesn't copy it word for word.

❸ Why use dialogue?

Dialogue breaks up the blocks of narrative (storytelling), and gives readers' eyes a rest. It increases the pace because it is quicker to read and it's a direct way of giving readers information.

❹ Creating atmosphere

Dialogue can be used to create different atmospheres. In *The Curse of the Gloamglozer*, the words of Linius Pallitax, the Most High Academe, create both immediate suspense and a sense of bad things to come:

> *"And close the door," Linius added.*
> *His voice dropped to an urgent whisper.*
> *"I don't want a single word of what*
> *I'm about to say to go beyond these four walls.*
> *Is that understood?"*
>
> Paul Stewart and Chris Riddell, *The Curse of the Gloamglozer*

❺ Evoke emotion

Go back to the *Dinosaur Summer* extract on page 69. The author Greg Bear (left) says a lot about the characters here. He tells us about Peter's life and his relationship with his mother. If you tried to write all this information as a piece of narrative, it would probably be three times as long. Peter's short answers show how he has learned to be wary of his parents' actions. His father reveals his contempt for his ex-wife's over-protectiveness. But it's Peter's sad little 'Oh' that makes us sympathize with him.

Now it's your turn

Talking with the enemy?

Write a short piece of dialogue between a human and an alien. One of them is pleading for his or her life. Decide whose point of view you are writing from. Try to find ways of indicating why one wants to exterminate the other. Make it humorous if you want to. Try to make the characters sound different from each other – an alien will not have the same speech patterns as a human even if they are speaking a common language. When you have finished, write the same thing as a piece of straight narrative, including the same information. Which version is the more interesting to read?

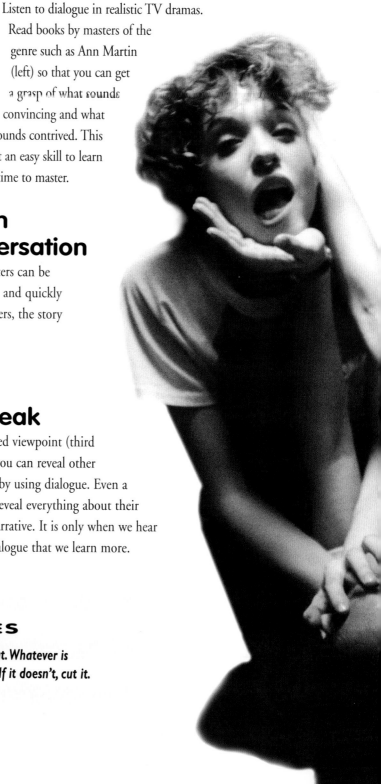

❻ Study other fiction writers

Listen to dialogue in realistic TV dramas. Read books by masters of the genre such as Ann Martin (left) so that you can get a grasp of what sounds convincing and what sounds contrived. This is not an easy skill to learn and will take time to master.

❼ Information through conversation

Conversations between characters can be used to push the story forward and quickly explain things about the speakers, the story or other characters.

❽ Let your characters speak

If you are writing from a limited viewpoint (third or first person), the only way you can reveal other character's opinions directly is by using dialogue. Even a first-person narrator may not reveal everything about their thoughts and feelings in the narrative. It is only when we hear them talking with others in dialogue that we learn more.

TIPS AND TECHNIQUES

Dialogue is never idle chitchat. Whatever is said must advance the story. If it doesn't, cut it.

In *The Illustrated Mum* by Jacqueline Wilson, narrator Dolphin presents herself as a lonely, dreamy girl who often has to help her mother Marigold through her bad times. But at school, where she is used to being shunned and ridiculed by Kayleigh and Yvonne, we see a much tougher side:

> *'Her mum!' said Yvonne.*
>
> *They all sniggered. My fists clenched.*
>
> *'Did you see her tattoos?' said Kayleigh.*
>
> *'All over her! My mum says tattoos are dead common,' said Yvonne.*
>
> *'Your mum's just jealous of my mum because she's a great fat lump like you,' I said, and shoved her hard in her wobbly stomach.*
>
> *'Um, you punched her!' said Kayleigh.*
>
> *'Yeah, and I'll punch you too,' I said, and I hit her hard, right on the chin.*
>
> *Then I marched out of the toilets, the other girls scattering in alarm.*
>
> Jacqueline Wilson, *The Illustrated Mum*

Now it's your turn

Spilling the beans ...

Write a conversation between your hero and a friend. The hero reveals something important – something they're ashamed of or angry about. The friend has to coax. Convey both characters' feelings. Find small ways to make them distinctive. Perhaps one has a pet expression?

9 Find different ways of speaking

Good dialogue can reveal what characters are really like. Speech patterns can show social status, education, regional origins and age, as well as suggesting the historical period.

10 Class differences

In *The Empty Sleeve*, Leon Garfield uses modern English, but shows 18th-century class differences in the ways characters address one another. Here the young locksmith's apprentice Peter Gannet meets Lord Marriner in the local tavern. The aristocrat calls Peter only by his master's name. In return, Peter speaks deferentially using a formal address, and also rather nervously, as the stammered 'y-yes' hints.

> *'You're Mr Woodcock's boy, aren't you?'*
> *said his lordship, kindly.*
>
> *'Y-yes, your lordship.'*
>
> *The waiter returned with the port.*
>
> *'Your health, Mr Woodcock's boy!'*
>
> Leon Garfield, *The Empty Sleeve*

11 Use accents

The extract opposite from *Arthur – The Seeing Stone* shows that Gatty has a country accent. The writer doesn't overdo it, just gives hints with 'why's and 'I can and all'. In *Underground to Canada*, Barbara Smucker gives the slave girl Julilly a rich turn of phrase that is interesting and easy to follow:

> *'You don't talk nasty like a snake's hiss,'* she giggled
> quietly. *'Something sure is different about today.'*
>
> Barbara Smucker, *Underground to Canada*

⑫ Evoke the past

Caroline Lawrence's *The Roman Mysteries* series has four very different main characters from Roman times: Flavia, the aristocrat; Jonathan, the outspoken Jewish doctor's son; Nubia, a freed African slave who struggles to speak formal Latin; and Lupus, a mute ex-street boy. The writer adds occasional words or phrases to suggest the period and the characters' backgrounds.

> *'Doctor Mordecai!' gasped Flavia. 'You look just like a Roman.'*
>
> *'Behold!' said Nubia. 'You have cut your hairs.'*
>
> *With his forefinger, Lupus pretended to shave his own smooth cheeks.*
>
> *'And shaved off your beard!' agreed Jonathan. 'Great Jupiter's eyebrows, father! Why did you do that?'*
>
> Caroline Lawrence, *The Roman Mysteries*

⑬ Education gap?

Arthur – The Seeing Stone is set in 12th-century England just before the Fourth Crusade. The quest for Jerusalem is on everyone's minds. Here, Gatty, a servant girl, shows her lack of education by asking Arthur, a scholarly lord's son, if Jerusalem is further away than the nearby English city of Chester:

> *'Much, much farther,' I said. 'Why?'*
>
> *'Why's because I want to see where Jesus was born. Instead of Ludlow fair, let's go to Jerusalem.'*
>
> *'Gatty!' I said. 'You can't walk to Jerusalem.'*
>
> *'I can and all,' said Gatty.*
>
> *'You can't,' I said. 'Only a magician could. It's across the sea.'*
>
> *Gatty lowered her head and looked at the ground. 'I didn't know that,' she said ...*
>
> Kevin Crossley Holland, *Arthur – The Seeing Stone*

Now it's your turn

Who's who?

Choose two characters from historical fiction who are different from each other in a particular way – perhaps one is richer, more educated or from a different place or social class. Invent a conversation between them. Think of ways to show their differences – both in their choice of words and in what they say.

⑭ Speak with shock

In Joyce Carol Oates' *Big Mouth and Ugly Girl*, Matt is taken by detectives to see the headmaster and is accused of trying to blow up his school:

> *Matt's teeth were chattering. He tried to speak calmly.*
> *'Look, this is crazy. I never ... what are you saying?'*
>
> *'We've had a report, Matt. Two reports. Two witnesses. They heard you.'*
>
> *'Heard me ... what?'*
>
> *'Threaten to "blow up the school".'*
>
> *Matt stared at the detective, uncomprehending.*
>
> *'Threaten to "massacre" as many people as you could. In the school cafeteria, just a few hours ago. Are you denying it?'*
>
> *'Y-yes! I'm denying it.'*
>
> *'You're denying it.'*
>
> *'I think this is all crazy.'*
>
> *'"This is all crazy." That's your response?'*

Joyce Carol Oates, *Big Mouth and Ugly Girl*

Now it's your turn

A family conversation

Write down a typical conversation between you and one of your parents. Try to capture exactly how they speak. What words or phrases do they habitually use that are different from yours? Rewrite it with a grandparent or elderly aunt speaking. Now think how your parents speak to their elders. Are there more differences?

⑮ Age differences

In *Artemis Fowl*, Eoin Colfer reverses the usual adult-talking-down-to-child pattern as young Artemis often speaks to the adult Butler as if he were the child. The following three lines give a snapshot of their unusual relationship:

> *'I hope this isn't another wild-goose chase, Butler,' Artemis said, his voice soft and clipped. 'Especially after Cairo.'*
> *'No, sir. I'm certain this time. Nguyen is a good man.'*
> *'Hmm,' droned Artemis, unconvinced.*

Eoin Colfer, *Artemis Fowl*

Now it's your turn

Pirate talk

Imagine you are eavesdropping on Captain Hook and Smee. They are discussing a host of different ways to kill Peter Pan and the Lost Boys. First make a list of a few nasty ideas they might come up with. Then think about Captain Hook and Smee as characters. They are both villains, but one is cruel and ferocious and the other more sly. Now write down their conversation, and see if you can give each character their own voice. Invent your own mannerisms for them if you want to. When you have finished, edit the piece, cutting out all unnecessary words. Then read it aloud and see if it flows. Make more improvements. Read it aloud again. Dialogue always takes a lot of rewriting.

BEATING WRITER'S BLOCK

Sometimes even the keenest writers can run out of words. This is called writer's block. It can last for days (or years!), but regular practise and lots of brainstorming will help. Here are some common causes:

❶ Get over your insecurities

Remember the Story Spectre from page 11 – your internal critic that belittles your work? Well give him the chop.
Do some timed brainstorming at once: the historical figures you'd most like to meet, your time machine's next destinations, how many words mean 'old', etc.

❷ Don't assume other writers are better than you

It is easy to believe that other writers are much better than you will ever be. Even experienced writers fall into this trap. But remember, the more you practise, the more you will improve. Remember! You may not become a successful novelist, but you could use your writing skills in other ways.

Case study

The poet Samuel Taylor Coleridge is one of the first known cases of writer's block. In 1804, he wrote: 'Yesterday was my Birth Day. So completely has a whole year passed, with scarcely the fruits of a month – O Sorrow and Shame. I have done nothing!'

Now it's your turn

Mystery time travel

In your next writing practice, imagine you are travelling in a time machine. It stops. The door opens. Step outside. Search for clues that tell you where you've landed. Are you pleased or petrified? Pour out your thoughts for ten minutes.

❸ Find fresh ideas

Thinking you have no ideas is a common block, but in history there are centuries' worth of stories waiting to be told. Visit your local museum or national museum (right) or a favourite historic place. Go out and search for a story.

❹ Coping with criticism

No one enjoys rejection or criticism, but it is an important part of learning to be a writer. If you invite someone to share your stories, be prepared for some negative comments. They may be more useful than flattery. See them as a reason to improve and rewrite your story if it really needs it.

❺ Understanding writer's block

The kind of writer's block that leaves you stuck mid-story, usually means there has not been enough planning. Maybe some horrible flaw in your plot has cropped up and looks like it might ruin everything. Don't panic! There will be an answer.

❻ Group brainstorming

If a key character (hero or villain) isn't coming to life, do some group brainstorming. Start by writing a brief character description at the top of a sheet of paper. When two minutes are up, pass it to a friend to add their ideas to yours. Don't worry about complete sentences. Thoughts are what count. Keep passing the paper round – the more friends willing to join in, the more ideas you will have. Mull over the results. Have you learned something about your character that you didn't know before?

❼ Compose a group story

Decide among you what the crime or mystery will be. Then everyone writes a character idea on a piece of paper, and drops it into a hat. Each person picks out a character at random and is responsible for developing that character and weaving them into the story. Did they commit the crime? What was their motive? Did they have the means and opportunity? To start, sit in a circle and take it in turns to develop the story. There are two rules: Speak your first thoughts and don't mind if others improve on your ideas. This is not about being clever. It's about shaping a story. The end result will be like a chapter synopsis, which you can develop later, either singly or together. But don't forget the all important story ingredients – problems, conflict and resolution.

Now it's your turn

Keep a journal

Write about life at school or home, record all the details of your hobbies and interests. Set yourself a minimum target length for each entry, say 300 words. If you use a computer for writing, you can count them easily. Make a note. Never write less than your target, even if it means describing the pattern of your bedroom wallpaper or what's in your sandwich. But try to write more. And look for ways of turning the day's events into an anecdote. Did your best friend have a row with her parents? Write about it. Write how you would feel if you were them.

❽ Use the news

Choose an interesting photo from a newspaper. If it's a place, make it the scene of the mystery. If it's a person, make them the subject of the mystery. Perhaps they have disappeared or been kidnapped. Pass the photo round the group. Everyone has to add their ideas about what has happened. Work out who did it, with what, why and how.

TIPS AND TECHNIQUES

If all else fails to spark inspiration and break that writer's block do something completely different. Walk the dog, clean out your bedroom. Doing tasks that give your mind a rest could be just the thing to spring an idea.

❾ Role play

Writing is a lonely activity, so why not turn your writing problem into a game with friends or family. Give them character roles to play and see what the dialogue between you conjures up.

❿ Ask 'What if?'

'What if?' is a good question to ask if your story isn't quite clear. What if my hero is really a nobleman's son, but doesn't realize it, like Oliver Twist (right) in Charles Dickens' book, seemingly condemned to life in the workhouse. What will he do if he finds out?

⓫ Interrogate your characters

If you still don't know your hero well enough to work out his or her story, you need to interrogate your character. Think again about what they look like, where they live, what emotions they feel, what they do for a living, what their strengths and weaknesses are, and who their friends and enemies are. To create well-rounded heroes, villains and supporting characters, you need to know these figures yourself inside out.

⓬ Keep a journal

If you keep a journal, you need never stop writing. When you visit museums and other historic places, be sure to record all your thoughts and impressions. These could provide valuable research ideas. Make sure you read what you have written regularly.

⑬ Be silly

If you still think you have absolutely nothing to say, try this. Give yourself ten minutes to describe the most boring, mind-numbing thing you can think of. Say how you survived the experience. Or maybe you didn't. Maybe it turned you into some other life form that just pretends to be you. Be funny, melodramatic, or downright ridiculous. Write it to entertain your friends.

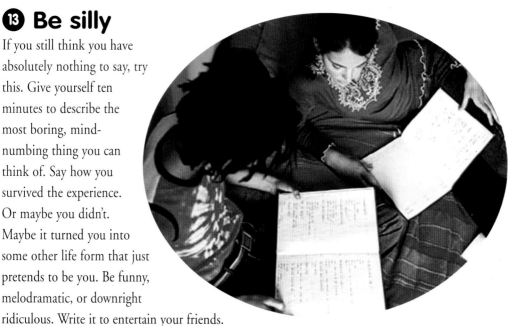

⑭ Tell someone else's story

If you really are stuck with your writing, try telling someone else's story. Retell a local legend or use Terry Jones' *The Lady and the Squire* back cover blurb on page 46 to write your own version of that story. The main thing is to finish it. Completing a piece of storytelling like this will spur you on with your own tales. Prove that you can finish something!

TIPS AND TECHNIQUES

Staring at a blank page, waiting for inspiration to strike, will only give you a headache and make you feel bad about yourself. Brainstorm a list. Write something. 'Something' can always be improved. 'Nothing' can't.

PREPARING YOUR WORK

Once you have finished your story, let it rest for a few weeks before you edit it. Then you will be able to see it with fresh eyes and spot any flaws more easily.

❶ Editing

Reading your work aloud will help you to simplify rambling sentences and clunky dialogue. Cut out all unnecessary adjectives and adverbs. Once you have cut down the number of words, decide how well the story works. Does it have a satisfying end? Has the hero resolved their problems? Now write it out afresh, or type it up on a computer. This is your manuscript.

❷ Think of a title

It is important to think up a good title; choose something intriguing and eye catching. Think about some titles you know and like.

❸ Be professional

Type the title on a title page, along with your name, address, telephone number and email address (repeat this information on the last page). Print the rest of your manuscript on single sides of A4 white paper, with wide margins and double line spacing. Pages should be numbered, and new chapters should start on a new page. This is what you need to do if you are sending it to a publisher, magazine or agent. But if you are sharing a story with family and friends, give it an attractive cover too.

TIPS AND TECHNIQUES

Whether you type up your story on a computer or do it by hand, always make a copy before you give it to anyone to read.

❹ Make your own book

If your school has its own publishing lab, why not use it to 'publish' your own story or to make a class story anthology (collection). A computer will let you choose your own font (print style) and justify the text (making even length margins like a professionally printed page). When you have typed and saved your story to a file, you can edit it quickly with the spell and grammar checker, or move sections of your story around using the 'cut and paste' facility, which saves a lot of rewriting. Having your story as a computer file also means you can print a copy whenever you need one, or revise the whole story if you want to.

Case study

Anne Fine writes all her stories in soft pencil that is easy to rub out. She ends up surrounded by rubbings. Even when she has finished a story, she does lots of revision and editing. It takes her about a year to write a children's book.

❺ Some places to publish your story

The next step is to find an audience for your story. Family members or classmates may be receptive. Or you may want to publish your work via a publishing house or online site. There are magazines and a number of writing websites that accept stories and novel chapters from young writers. Some have chat rooms and some give writing advice too and run regular competitions. Each site has its own rules about submitting work to them, so make sure you read them carefully before you send in a story.

You can also:

• Send things to your school magazine, or if your school doesn't have a magazine, then start your own with like-minded friends.

• Keep your eyes peeled when reading your local newspaper or your favourite comics and magazines. They might be running a writing competition that you can submit something to.

• Keep an eye open at local museums and colleges. Some run creative writing workshops during school holidays.

❻ Writing clubs

Starting a writing club or critique group and exchanging stories is a great way of getting your stories out there. It will also get you used to criticism from others, which will prove invaluable in learning how to write. Your local library might be kind enough to provide a forum for such a club.

❼ Finding a publisher

Secure any submission with a paperclip and always enclose a short letter (saying what you have sent) and a stamped, addressed envelope for the story's return. Study the market and find out which publishing houses are most likely to publish your type of fiction. Addresses of publishing houses and information about whether they accept submissions can be found in writers' handbooks. Bear in mind that manuscripts that haven't been asked for or paid for by a publisher – unsolicited submissions – are rarely published.

❽ Some famous rejections

Even though Allen & Unwin had successfully published Tolkien's *The Hobbit* in 1936, they rejected *The Lord of the Rings* at first, thinking adults wouldn't read a hobbit book. It had taken Tolkien over ten years to write. L. Frank Baum had his *The Wonderful Wizard of Oz* story rejected by the Hill Company because the publishers didn't like the original title, *The Emerald City*. They thought it unlucky. If the difficulties of having your work published make you downhearted, have faith. If you really want to be a published writer, you will find a way.

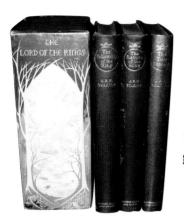

❾ Writer's tip

If your story is rejected by an editor, see it as a chance to make it better. Try again! But remember ... having your work published is wonderful, but it is not the only thing. Being able to make up a story is a gift, so why not give yours to someone you love? Read it to a younger brother or sister. Tell it to your grandmother. Find your audience!

Case study

Philip Pullman began his storytelling career as a child. He loved comics and used to make up his own stories to tell his younger brother and friends. After a time he began to write his own stories down.

WHEN YOU'VE FINISHED YOUR STORY

Completing your first story is a wonderful achievement. You have started to master your writer's craft and probably learned a lot about yourself too. But now, you must seek out another quest. You have several options.

❶ How about a sequel?

When thinking about your next work, ask yourself: 'Can I write a sequel and develop the story?' Each *Harry Potter* book, for example, is a complete story, but the characters and the conflicts with Voldemort continue and develop from book to book.

J. K. Rowling (left) gives a summary of Harry's backstory near the start of her books, so that if someone reads one out of order, they can still understand and enjoy the story. She planned to have a seven-book series right from the start: a book for each year of Harry's training at Hogwarts.

❷ Trilogies

Paul Stewart and Chris Riddell's elaborate universe in *The Edge Chronicles* simply demands to have more tales told of it. Trilogies mirror the beginning-middle-end of a single

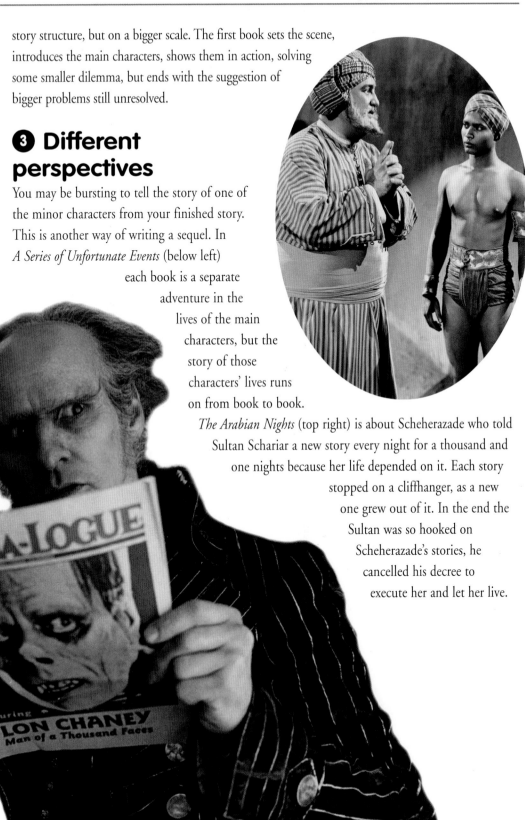

story structure, but on a bigger scale. The first book sets the scene, introduces the main characters, shows them in action, solving some smaller dilemma, but ends with the suggestion of bigger problems still unresolved.

❸ Different perspectives

You may be bursting to tell the story of one of the minor characters from your finished story. This is another way of writing a sequel. In *A Series of Unfortunate Events* (below left) each book is a separate adventure in the lives of the main characters, but the story of those characters' lives runs on from book to book.

The Arabian Nights (top right) is about Scheherazade who told Sultan Schariar a new story every night for a thousand and one nights because her life depended on it. Each story stopped on a cliffhanger, as a new one grew out of it. In the end the Sultan was so hooked on Scheherazade's stories, he cancelled his decree to execute her and let her live.

aturing
LON CHANEY
Man of a Thousand Faces

❹ Off on a tangent?

Perhaps while you were writing the first story, an idea started simmering in your mind. Perhaps you made a few notes in your 'ideas' file. Do those ideas still excite you? Go back to the start of this book and repeat some of the brainstorming exercises to help you develop the idea further.

❺ A famous example

Sometimes a hero is so intriguing and pushy that they demand more tales about them. Joan Aiken's Dido Twite is just such a character. This brave, smart-talking, smart-thinking Cockney waif first appeared in *Black Hearts in Battersea* (a sequel to *The Wolves of Willoughby Chase*), only to be lost at sea at the end of the book. But in *Nightbirds in Nantucket* she comes sailing back aboard Captain Coffin's whaler and is soon set to foil another wicked Hanoverian plot.

❻ Keep researching

Keep looking for stories: visit a museum, look through history books, learn about a specific invention, read the diary of a real or fictional person or nag a grandparent for family stories.

Joan Lowery Nixon got the idea for her stories this way. She wanted to 'bring history and fiction together in an exciting, adventurous time and place, to tell the stories of those who could have travelled west on the orphan train.' Nixon wrote more than 140 books during her prestigious career. She was first published at ten years old. Her works include *The Kidnapping of Christina Lattimore* and *A Place to Belong*. Here are her tips: Suspense calls for the emotional responses of anxiety, excitement and fear. Make a list of clues that you can use in your story. One should be the crucial clue that helps the main character finally solve the mystery.

Now it's your turn

Can a minor become a major?

Often it is a story's minor character that steals the show. They may only appear briefly, but create maximum impact. Often at the end of the story you are left pondering their fate. Just like TV, these minor characters can sometimes get a spin-off show of their own. In your case, this minor character could become your hero or villain in their own story. Gollum was a wonderful character J. R. R. Tolkien created for *The Hobbit*, although he does not appear for long. But Gollum was too interesting not to use again and in *The Lord of the Rings* he has a pivotal role, helping to seal the fate of Middle Earth. If you think one of your minor characters could become a major one, follow the brainstorming exercise on page 49.

TIPS AND TECHNIQUES

Remember, to become a creative writer you must read, read, read; write, write, write, write.

blurb – publisher's description on a book jacket that persuades you to read the book.

chapter synopsis – an outline describing briefly what is happening in each chapter.

cliché – a worn-out idea/description/plot, e.g. 'white as snow' is a cliché.

cliffhanger – ending a chapter or switching viewpoint at a nail-biting moment.

editing – removing all unnecessary words from your story and making it the best it can be.

editor – the person who works in a publishing house and finds new books to publish. They also advise authors on how to improve their storytelling methods by telling them what needs adding or cutting.

first-person viewpoint – stories told in the first person and describing only what that person experiences, e.g. 'It was July when I left for Timbuktu. Just the thought of going back there made my heart sing.'

foreshadowing – dropping hints of coming events or dangers that are essential to the outcome of the story.

genre – a particular type of writing, e.g. fantasy, historical, adventure, science fiction are all examples of different genres.

imagery – making word pictures. *See also* metaphor *and* simile.

internal critic – the voice inside your head that picks holes in your work and makes you want to give up writing.

light relief – a scene of lighter or humorous mood used to give readers a rest from too much suspense/action/drama.

list – the list of book titles that a publisher has already published or is about to publish.

manuscript – your story when it is written down, either typed or by hand.

metaphor – calling a man a 'mouse' is a metaphor. It is a word picture. From it we learn in one word that the man is timid or pathetic, not that he is actually a mouse.

motivation – the reason why a character does something.

narrative – adjective: telling the story; noun: the story.

omniscient viewpoint – the all-knowing eye that sees all the characters and tells readers how they are acting and feeling.

plagiarism – copying someone else's work and passing it off as your own; it is a serious offence.

plot – the sequence of events that drives a story forwards.

point of view (POV) – the eyes through which a story is told.

sequel – a story that carries an existing one forwards.

simile – saying something is like something else. It is a word picture, e.g. 'clouds like frayed lace'.

slush pile – the collection of unsolicited synopses and stories sent to a publisher.

synopsis – a short summary that describes what a story is about and introduces the main characters.

theme – the main idea that is explored in the story such as war or slavery, or human values such as courage and justice. A story may have several themes.

third-person viewpoint – stories told in the third person, which only show events from that character's viewpoint.

unsolicited submission – sending a book or story to a publisher without being asked. These submissions usually end up in the slush pile.

writer's block – when writers think they can no longer write.

• Ask for a subscription to magazines such as *Cricket* and *Cicada* for your birthday. Or find them in your library. They publish the very best in young people's short fiction and you can learn your craft and read great stories at the same time. *Cicada* also accepts submissions from its subscribers. www.cricketmag.com

• Make a good friend of your local librarian. They can direct you to useful sources of information that you might not have thought of. They will also know of any published author scheduled to speak in your area.

• Get your teacher to invite a favourite author to speak at your school.

Places to submit your stories and other useful websites

The magazine *Stone Soup* accepts stories and artwork from 8- to 13-year-olds. Their website is www.stonesoup.com

The Young Writers Club is an Internet-based club where you can post your stories. Check them out at: www.youngwritersclub.com

Young Writer at www.young-writer.co.uk and other similar sites at www.kidsreads.com for 6- to-18-year-olds.

www.kidpub.com is a subscription club that posts 40,000 young people's stories 'from all over the planet'.

Writing links on Kids on the Net:
www.kidsonthenet.org.uk

To learn more about mysteries and mystery writing check out:
http://kids.MysteryNet.com

For general writing advice see author Aaron Shepherd's site:
www.aaronshep.com/storytelling

Historical sources

For details of everyday life, the Costume Page (www.costumepage.org) has excellent links to sites that deal with dress through the ages.

For British history see www.bbc.co.uk/history and www.channel4.com/history

For American history visit the Library of Congress American Memory Site at www.memory.loc.gov/ammem